A
DAUGHTER'S
GEOGRAPHY

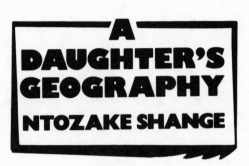

A DAUGHTER'S GEOGRAPHY
NTOZAKE SHANGE

St. Martin's Press/New York

Design by Manuela Paul

Library of Congress Cataloging in Publication Data

Shange, Ntozake.
    A daughter's geography.

    I. Title.
PS3569.H3324D3   1983   811'.54   83-9625
ISBN 0-312-18342-9
ISBN 0-312-18343-7 (lim. ed.)

First Edition
10 9 8 7 6 5 4 3 2 1

For My Daughter, Savannah Thulani Éloisa & our grandmothers
    Eloise Owens Williams & Martha Binion
        Viola Benzena Murray Owens & Ida B. Williams
For our godmothers
    Thulani Davis, Jessica Hagedorn, Nanette Bearden, Gail
        Merrifield, Margaret Sullivan, & Katie Moore
my sisters/ her aunts
    Wanda 'Ifa' Williams & Bisa Elise Williams-Manigault
my brother/ her uncle
    Paul Towbin Williams, Esq.
for my father / her grandfather 'Boppy' Paul T. Williams. M.D.
her detroit grandfather with his mighty prayers
    Rev. Earl Binion
our cousins 2nd, 3rd, 4th, 5th, 6th, from New York to Texas &
        Detroit
    whom we know & love

Ahora que tu has ruelto
de recio de humo
lágrima y lágrima

Y que es tu vas apenas
laúd, metal lejano
lágrima y lágrima

De tu cintura hacen
las siempremas
lágrima y lágrima

Una paloma oscura
me persigue y te nambia

Lágrima. Lágrimas.

—Rafaela Chacon Nardi
(Martinez Inoforza
Editorial Letras Cubanas
Ciudad de La Habana, Cuba, 1982)

Contents

It Hasnt Always Been This Way

for
Eubie Blake
Duke Ellington
James van der Zee

i. Mood Indigo

it hasnt always been this way
ellington was not a street
robeson no mere memory
du bois walked up my father's stairs
hummed some tune over me
sleeping in the company of men
who changed the world

it wasnt always like this
why ray barretto used to be a side-man
& dizzy's hair was not always grey
i remember   i was there
i listened in the company of men
politics as necessary as collards
music even in our dreams

our house was filled with all kinda folks
our windows were not cement or steel
our doors opened like our daddy's arms
held us safe & loved
children growing in the company of men
old southern men & young slick ones
sonny til was not a boy
the clovers no rag-tag orphans
our crooners/ we belonged to a whole world
nkrumah was no foreigner
virgil aikens was not the only fighter

it hasnt always been this way
ellington was not a street

ii. Improvisation

𝄢 11's

there is something caught in my throat
it is this place
my baby is sleeping
i check to see if she is alive
she does not know about gagging
she does not have this place/ in her throat
she doesnt know where we are
how it sears the membranes
eats the words right outta your mouth
leaves you suckin' pollutants impotence
& failure/

      a whole race of people cant do nothin'
at the roller disco.

𝄞 7/8

there is something caught in my throat
it is hard & ugly/ i wd vomit it out
but the malignancy only grows toward
my gut/ & will not come out alive
my child is sleeping
she doesnt know where we are &
some man/ wants to kiss my thighs
roll his tongue around my navel
put his hands all up my ass
& this place is in my throat

△ 14

𝄢 5/4

how can i tell him
there is nothing up my behind/ that
will get this place
out of my throat.
(i went to a dangerous place with a man who
was not there/ cuz he cant do nothin' but
dial-a-joke or call for information)

i cd tell him a few things
there are dead children out here
there are desperate women out here
the sky is falling
& i am choking to death
cuz of where i am & who we are.

 9/15

this is the twentieth century.
(do you think artra skin tone cream will solve the
colored complexion problem during a limited nuclear
engagement/ or
are you stocking up on porcelana?)

 6/8

i have this thing in my throat
i cant put no more tongues in my mouth/
no cigarettes/ no tranquilizers/ i cant eat anything
i shoulda kept my damn champagne.

& asked the coke man for something so good/
it would burn this place
outta my soul/ so i cd breathe
& check my daughter who is still sleeping

 3/4

she thinks unicorns & magnolias
are things to put in her mouth
she dont know where she is yet
she dont know alla black kid's gonna get
is a fist in her mouth or a white man
who says she's arrogant/ cuz
she can look him in the eye/ cuz
she dont know where she is.

𝄞 4/4

this thing is in my throat/
exploding just beneath my chin
i told this man my daughter didnt know
where she was/ where i keep my child
there are no white men with sexual thoughts
about infants/ she'll know better next time
cuz she aint having this place
this gun happy/ watch niggers die/ fuck
each other to death in style/ when
they got ads sayin' Come & See The Satin Latins / but you gotta

dress as white gods & goddesses/
she aint here for that.

 13/15

i am choking to death
             (& some man watched me looking for him
             in the rain & called me later to say
             he saw me in the rain/ looking & couldnt
             do anything about it cuz it was an
             aesthetic thing)
this place is caught in my throat
i would tear it out & let you eat it
but i have a daughter who sleeps well/ & till
somebody comes to help me/ i'll have to keep
swallowing this place/ like the rest of you
praying i wont have to hold
all my respect for human beings in my one closed fist
my one fistfull of fight/ that we'll choke
on this place/ & make it somewhere
we could live.

             please
             dont send no flowers.
             i dont want no white wine.
             i dont even want a roof over my head.
i want this place out of my throat
i want james brown to stop singing/ to get the hell out the way
& let a man come in.

△ 17

iii. Take the A Train

i could sleep with a man
but i'll lay with the souls of black folks
maybe i could grow me something
some azure flower that would smell
like life to me/ a root of some healing spice
might push up from my soils/ if i
dream with the souls of black folks.

what is invisible is not a man
but the spirits of some who were
bigger is not a black boy yearning for an airplane
but the gaze of our children who dont know
why 'we caint get no satisfaction.'

i could sleep with a man
i could even sing with a man
but i gotta rise with the souls of black folks
where could the A train take me
if i dont know where i'm sposed to go
ellington is not a street.
       & my child knows her world
       is as rich as *people in sorrow* can spare/
       brash as our bodies in the *black forest*

but it hasnt always been this way
i swear/ we were not always missing.

Bocas: A Daughter's Geography

for
Savannah
Thulani
Éloisa

Bocas: A Daughter's Geography

i have a daughter/ mozambique
i have a son/ angola
our twins
salvador & johannesburg/ cannot speak
the same language
but we fight the same old men/ in the new world

we are so hungry for the morning
we're trying to feed our children the sun
but a long time ago/ we boarded ships/ locked in
depths of seas our spirits/ kisst the earth
on the atlantic side of nicaragua costa rica
our lips traced the edges of cuba puerto rico
charleston & savannah/ in haiti
we embraced &
made children of the new world
but old men spit on us/ shackled our limbs
but for a minute
our cries are the panama canal/ the yucatan
we poured thru more sea/ more ships/ to manila
ah ha we're back again
everybody in manila awready speaks spanish

the old men sent for the archbishop of canterbury
"can whole continents be excommunicated?"
"what wd happen to the children?"
"wd their allegiance slip over the edge?"
"dont worry bout lumumba/ don't even think bout
ho chi minh/ the dead cant procreate"
so say the old men

but i have a daughter/ la habana
i have a son/ guyana
our twins
santiago & brixton/ cannot speak
the same language
yet we fight the same old men

the ones who think helicopters rhyme with hunger
who think patrol boats can confiscate a people
the ones whose dreams are full of none of our
children
they see mae west & harlow in whittled white cafes
near managua/ listening to primitive rhythms in
jungles near pétionville
with bejeweled benign natives
ice skating in abidjan
unaware of the rest of us in chicago
all the dark urchins
rounding out the globe/ primitively whispering
the earth is not flat old men

there is no edge
no end to the new world
cuz i have a daughter/ trinidad
i have a son/ san juan
our twins
capetown & palestine/ cannot speak the same
language/ but we fight the same old men
the same men who thought the earth waz flat
go on over the edge/ go on over the edge old men

you'll see us in luanda. or the rest of us
in chicago
rounding out the morning/
we are feeding our children the sun

Tween Itaparica & Itapuã

itaparica is where doña flor
took her two husbands/ itaparica is where
giorgio dos santos is nine years fulla mosquito bites
& will die soon
itaparica is not near corcuvado
       cristo redentor
nor the/ copacabana
where the children eat off the plates of tourists/
anything/ no
itaparica is not close to rocinha
behind the sheraton/ covered with tin, stolen
bricks & women's stooped shoulders
i know rocinha's the only favela
with a legal city sign:

    IPANEMA
    LEME
    COPACABANA
    ROCINHA

& a real city bus/ past the churrascurias of mud
in cidade dos santos/ the city of saints
thru gamblers of liberdade/ the barrio of liberty
the children of manguera comin back with hands fulla
rice/ thrown off chicken bones . . .
this is not close to itaparica

itaparica is an island/ near salvador
where my mother sat on a cannon
that usedta guard slave ships comin to the New World
ao mundo novo/ my father got his 17th century feet back
walkin on hot cobblestones
some bahiano laid in this heat
bahiano africano pretu moreno mulatto
some one of us laid this/ we are walkin/
it is still hot round the curve of our heels
itaparica where service is such an industry aos garçoms
take their time/ there is no where else/

itaparica is an island
a half-day's sail from salvador
one half-hour of itapuã
where the old man fries fish & counts money
                in his favor
his children row boats like in mindanao
like in mindanao/ they have forgotten
nothing

itapuã with a church on the highest hill
like land houses in curaçao
the safest place for slave owners
on crests of waves of slaves
who cd not move without being seen

our lady of lourdes in jurujuba
collects crutches & back braces
itapuã collects tourists

throws them back to the sea
under the gaze of the master of christ's house/
tween itaparica & itapuã

i found a calm
a rinsing off of history too grimy
a washing away of memories not fit for sleep
a burnin salted cleansing
i sailed/ i sailed on a schooner
smelling of fish/ whiskey & sweat

i sailed to a samba
slept with the sea in a fit of petulance
consorted with winds rough as avenue 'c'
you climbed from those stars
tween itaparica & itapuã

you sat up in the sky/ began to strut around
yr legs swept thru the night/ you took the
half-moon in yr hands/ twirled her
a pinwheel/ for me
you settled on a armful of stars
took me to a harbor

some visions slip outta trees
others stalk the lakes inland
others leap from the glory of the sun
you stood up in the night/ yr palms pushing stars
to fall in delirium/ letting me know
all i see is true
we are as impregnable as night/ as dangerous

i sailed to a samba
tween itaparica & itapuã
you walked across the sky
to give me safe harbor

i slept with the sea in a fit of petulance
you climbed from the stars
in yr new straw hat
tween itaparica & itapuã

You Are Sucha Fool

you are sucha fool/ i haveta love you
you decide to give me a poem/ intent on it/ actually
you pull/ kiss me from 125th to 72nd street/ on
the east side/ no less
you are sucha fool/ you gonna give me/ the poet/
the poem
insistin on proletarian images/ we buy okra/
3 lbs for $1/ & a pair of 98¢ shoes
we kiss
we wrestle
you make sure at east 110th street/ we have cognac
no beer all day
you are sucha fool/ you fall over my day like
a wash of azure

you take my tongue outta my mouth/
make me say foolish things
you take my tongue outta my mouth/ lay it on yr skin
like the dew between my legs
on this the first day of silver balloons
& lil girl's braids undone
friendly savage skulls on bikes/ wish me good-day
you speak spanish like a german & ask puerto rican
marketmen on lexington if they are foreigners

oh you are sucha fool/ i cant help but love you
maybe it was something in the air
our memories
our first walk
our first . . .
yes/ alla that

where you poured wine down my throat in rooms
poets i dreamed abt seduced sound & made history/
you make me feel like a cheetah
a gazelle/ something fast & beautiful
you make me remember my animal sounds/
so while i am an antelope
ocelot & serpent speaking in tongues
my body loosens for/ you

you decide to give me the poem
you wet yr fingers/ lay it to my lips
that i might write some more abt you/
how you come into me
the way the blues jumps outta b.b. king/ how
david murray assaults a moon & takes her home/
like dyanne harvey invades the wind

oh you/ you are sucha fool/
you want me to write some more abt you
how you come into me like a rollercoaster in a
dip that swings
leaving me shattered/ glistening/ rich/ screeching
& fully clothed

you set me up to fall into yr dreams
like the sub-saharan animal i am/ in all this heat
wanting to be still
to be still with you
in the shadows
all those buildings
all those people/ celebrating/ sunlight & love/ you

you are sucha fool/ you spend all day piling up images
locations/ morsels of daydreams/ to give me a poem

just smile/ i'll get it

Oh, I'm 10 Months Pregnant

i tried to tell the doctor
i really tried to tell her
tween the urine test & the internal exam/
when her fingers were circling my swollen cervix
i tried
to tell her the baby was confused
the baby doesnt know
she's not another poem.

you see/ i was working on a major piece of fiction
at the time of conception
"doctor/ are you listening?"
had just sent 4 poems off to the *new yorker*
& was copy-editing a collection of plays
during those "formative first twelve weeks"
there were numerous opening parties
all of which involved me & altered the poor baby's
amniotic bliss/
      "doctor/ the baby doesnt think she shd
      come out that way!"

i mean/ she thinks she shd come up/ not down
into the ground/ she thinks her mother makes up things
nice things ugly things but made up things nonetheless
unprovable irrational subjective fantastic things
not subject to objective or clinical investigation/
she believes the uterine cave is a metaphor
      "doctor/ you have to help me"

this baby wants to jump out of my mouth
at a reading someplace/

the baby's refusing to come out/ down
she wants to come out a spoken word
& i have no way to reach her/she is
no mere choice of words/how can i convince her
to drop her head & take on the world like the rest of us
she cant move up till she comes out
           "whatever shall i do? I've been pregnant
           a long time"

i finally figured out what to say
to this literary die-hard of a child of mine
"you are an imperative my dear"/ & i felt her startle
toward my left ovary then I said/ "as an imperative
it is incumbent upon you to present yrself"

A Black Night in Haiti, Palais National, Port-au-Prince

the sailor/ le marin/ tells me
"there is no violence in haiti.
   jamaica has so many problems
the black people here are 'la majorité.' "
the children are begging
   "lady give me something"
they make his heart sick
he sails yachts for italians hiding from the red brigade
he thinks i'm cute & exotic/ even
i think of brazilians/ on emancipation
sailing back to dahomey/ he sails yachts
from capetown to rio/ charters for the french
americans have so lil class
the begging children make his heart sick

dessalines/ are the women sleeping at yr feet
bothersome/ does yr marble horse smell their fatigue
the mensis & milk at noon
the old man with one leg/ one hand/ one
elbow/ does he offend yr
sensibilities

on these great marble horses
will you come again/ some one of you
sweep thru the alleys & the stink/ come here
with yr visions
la liberté. l'égalité. la fraternité.
come visit among us that we might know
again/ some hope

port-au-prince is a rough town
le boulevard jean-jacques dessalines
a desecration/ *les haitiennes* paint
like niggahs in philadelphia love to dance/
all over the roads/ paradise jumps
from canvas/ to be sold to tourists/ to take abroad

pétion/ l'ouverture/ dessalines
on horseback/ will you ride back
thru here/ invoke those same spirits
you called on at the citadel/ there are half-naked
women sleeping at yr feet/ children begging under yr
bridled stallions/ what 3 horses wd balk at/ one black man
carries on his back/ his sweat falls into the streams
of blood/ the yng men spit up
on le boulevard jean-jacques dessalines

papa doc made it possible
duvalier hadda lotta ju ju hoodoo grisgris
weapons
duvalier insisted/ the black people
cd go everywhere
aux téâtres/ aux restaurants/ aux musées/ to hell
his son lights up le palais national like christmas
in new york/ every night
the secret police come out in their trucks/ to scour
nos voisins/ our neighborhoods
can you stand it?
can you stand it, dessalines?
can you stand it, pétion/ l'ouverture?
can you stand these children

with the red eyes & dacron brazzieres for sale?
do you believe all the prostitutes/ in la fiesta/ el barrio
are from santo domingo/ des vaches espagnoles?/ vacas
des vaches espagnoles?

now/ marius trésor is an international hero
he plays soccer & sleeps with a blonde
do you ride yr horses for him?
do you salute the deformed of port-au-prince
with yr plumed hats & swords?
what are you doing on those goddamned horses?
cant you see these old women hobbling abt
like mares abt to be shot/ leaning on fences
by the palais national where
jean-claude invokes the spirits & disgraces
le negre marron who awready ran away from slavery
in santo domingo/ to catch the tears
of these children/ who have so lil will
they dont even steal . . .
dessalines/ pétion/ l'ouverture
you must come back
start all over again
no one will move
personne ne bouge pas sans la puissance des dieux
vous les connaissez/ venez ici
tes enfants ne savent que la mort
tes femmes marchent avec la faim
tes hommes travaillent sans raison
tes vieux sont fatigués
what are you doing on those marble horses?

l'haiti a besoin
l'haiti a besoin/ de la liberté/ l'égalité/ fraternité.
l'haiti/ le premier pays au monde/ sans esclaves
l'haiti/la nation de l'indépendance noire
what is going on/ here?
où est dessalines/ maintenant?
où est pétion/ l'ouverture?
où sont-ils qui peuvent nous aider à la liberté
l'égalité/ la fraternité?
où sont-ils maintenant/ l'haiti a besoin
where are you now?
haiti's in need . . .

Some Men

i.

some/ men
dont know anything abt that
the manliness inherent at birth
is lost as they grow or shrink
to size

some/ men
dont know that a well dressed man
is a good female impersonator
that machines replace them & do a better job

some/ men
have no language that doesn't hurt
a language that doesn't reduce what's whole
to some part of nothing

sometimes/ some men think
it's funny/ really funny
women have anything to do with them

ii.

he was a pretty man who liked pretty things.
surrounded with beat-up luxuries/ old mantillas
from women's heads lay cross his mahogany tables/
bronze nymphs, bulbs in their mouths, lit up
his quarters/ onyx vases steadied scarlet tulips before
french windows he opened when he had espresso
in early morning.
he kept a dressing gown/ mauve dotted with black velvet.
he waxed his floors til they shone & covered them with

near eastern rugs/ the kind little girls spend whole
lives tying.
he walked about grandly.
though he was a little man/ he liked to think himself
                    large.
he had so many pretty things.
he never bent his knees/ that added some inches
& kept him from looking anyone in the eye
            there'd be nothing new in his visions. only
old pretty things/ used abused beauties
like the women who decorated his bed from time to time.
he sat them on old sheets & displayed the dusty
manuscripts he collected/ the vintage photographs
he stored/ the women past whose legs he'd pulled
over his hips like a holster.
            now this was an honor
to lay naked with a pretty man among his pretty things/
the violated thrown-out pieces of lives he recovered
from rummages scavenging & gutters.
the beauty of it all
was it cost him so little. imagine him
so small a man getting away with all that.
            nothing new. not a new thing.

what's to value in something unblemished?
porcelain must be cracked/ to covet. rugs frayed/
to desire. there must be scratches on the surfaces/
to enjoy what's beautiful.

he was really very tiny in the big brass bed.
the beauty of the woman overpowered him. she didn't

even seem afraid in the presence of all his
pretty things.
he thought of the most beautiful thing he cd say.
what words wd match his pretty little face.
what phrase approach the sunlight mad with joy
on the limbs of this woman next to him.
what he could do so perfectly.
he was a little man
& straightening his legs in the bed added nothing to
his stature. he sat up & crushed the frailty of the morning
        "suck my dick & make some coffee"
he squealed.

she ran out
with no more than her coat/ her shoes in her hands
keys in her mouth. she thought she must have lost
her mind.
but
he was a small man
& cd handle only damaged goods. he sat in his big bed
with his little legs bent/ quite content.
now/ there was something someone else cd collect/
an abused/ used luxury/ a woman
with a memory of daybreak in a near perfect place/
sunlight warm against her face & a man squealing
suck my dick & make some coffee
        SUCK MY DICK & MAKE SOME COFFEE
she always woke before her lovers/ after that.
she never slept near windows/ & the aroma of coffee
left her pale.

if she lived empty & angular as he did, she'd become
less a woman & part of the design/ where anything he
wanted to happen/ happened.

vii.

the baby gets up every hour & a half. she's a spunky
little baby who cries & smiles a lot. she needs to nurse
& her mama's right there. without sleep or no/ the milk flows.
            he doesn't like that. he said.
there's no one taking care of me. he thought
her stitches shd heal faster. she shdn't take so
many sitz baths. she takes too long to walk from here to
there/ she doesnt actually haveta walk funny like that
it dont hurt her/ it wont hurt/ he said/ it wdnt hurt.
dont you remember before that damned baby? it was me.
it was me & you. there's always milk for the baby
none for me/ never too tired for the baby/ never too
tired for the baby/ he didn't understand
why she sat on the stairway crying all night with the
spunky little baby
he hadnt done nothing but hold her arms back/ & bite
on her titties/ how did he know his teeth wd hurt
how cd he know/ shit/ she always has time for the baby
what was he sposed to do/ the milk flows whether she tired
or not/ when was he gonna get some/ he said it wont hurt/
it wont hurt/ dont you remember . . .

viii.
he waited
        til she got out of her car
& pulled his dick out   exactly 6 ft
from her doorway.
            the car was locked
            the front door was locked
there was a man with his dick out
freezin winds
her hands trembling/ her mouth falling over her scalp
his laughter came all over her coat

ix.
he looked at the flowers on her window sill/
roses, lilacs, lilies & mums. the flowers
on her curtains/ blazing tropical petals
& stamen
her desk festooned with strange cacti & terrarium.
she had covered her ceilings in arcs of ivy/
made herself a garden full of soft round shapes/
fragrance & manners.
he felt her thighs/ strong & wet.
her body arching like ferns reaching/ she was smiling
& feverish with desire
            strange sounds fell from her mouth
gurgling innocent hot sounds/ crept along his back
her fingers
sought out the hairs long his neck/
the evening fog laced kisses round their bodies/

she thought she heard piano solos/ she thought she heard
trumpets gone marvelously wild in nature's murmurings
                she felt him coming
& let go all her powers
when without warning
he shot all his semen up her ass
        she kept screaming
WHAT ARE YOU DOING WHAT ARE YOU DOING to me
he relaxed/ sighing
            "i had to put it somewhere. it was
too good to be some pussy."

X.

some men would rather see us dead than imagine
what we think of them/
if we measure our silence by our pain
how could all the words
any word
ever catch us up
what is it
we cd call equal.

About Atlanta

cuz he's black & poor
he's disappeared
the name waz lost   the games werent played
nobody tucks him in at night/ wipes traces
of cornbread & syrup from his fingers
the corners of his mouth
cuz he's black & poor/ he's not
just gone
disappeared one day
& his blood soaks up what's awready red
in atlanta

no ropes this time   no tar & feathers
werent no parades of sheets fires & crosses
nothing/ no signs

empty bunkbeds
mothers who forget & cook too much on sundays
just gone/ disappeared
cuz he's black & poor   he's gone
took a bus/ never heard from again

but somebody heard a child screaming
        & went right on ahead
children disappearing/ somewhere in the woods/ decaying
just gone/ disappeared/ in atlanta

mothers are always at the window watching
caint nobody disappear right in fronta yr eyes

but who knows what we cd do
when we're black & poor
we aint here no way/ how cd we disappear?
who wd hear us screaming?

say it was a man with a badge & some candy
say it was a man with a badge & some money
say it was a maniac
cd be more n sticks n stones
gotta be more than stars n stripes
children caint play war when they in one.
caint make believe they dyin/ when they are
caint imagine what they'll be/ cuz they wont
just gone/ disappeared

oh mary dont you weep & dont you moan
oh mary dont you weep & dont you moan
HOLLAR i say HOLLAR
cuz we black & poor & we just disappear

we cant find em   jesus cant find em
til they seepin in soil
father reekin in soil
they bones bout disappeared
they lives aint never been
bleeding where the earth's awready red
dyin cuz they took a bus
& mama caint see that far out her window

the front porch dont go from here to eternity
& they gone
just disappeared

but somebody heard them screaming
somebody crushed them children's bones
somebody's walkin who shd be crawling
for killing who aint never been
cuz we black & poor/ we just be gone

no matter how sweet/ no matter how quiet
just gone
be right back ma
going to the store mother dear
see ya later nana
call ya when i get there mama
& the soil runs red with our dead in atlanta
cuz somebody went right on ahead
crushing them lil bones/ strangling them frail wails
cuz we black & poor
our blood soaks up dirt
while we disappearing

mamas keep looking out the door
saying "i wonder where is my child/ i wonder
        where is my child"
she dont turn the bed back cuz she knows
we black & poor
& we just disappear/ be gone

oh mary dont you weep & dont you moan
oh mary dont you weep & dont you moan
i wonder where is my child
i wonder where is my child

nothing/ no signs
in atlanta

Hijo de las Americas

i must go to La Costa/ on the Atlantic side/
where the English left Nicaragua black & poor.
carlos, cherry brown, in a afro/ keeps us
up in the night under Sandino's light/ reading
poems recovered from the war/ small pieces of paper
left at someone's house/ small typed pages that cd fit
in his shoe/ Somoza *jailed* poets *killed* poets *maimed* poets.

there is something from the war / still
hurting carlito's leg/ he cannot stand in line for his lunch
he reads all night of the black coal-miners gold-miners
choking on dust/ having no future that is not
another black hole in the ground.
carlos reads the poems he can/ the rest
were *burned* by friends/ when the security police
la guardia nacional/ came looking for a free black
mind/ *burned* poems cannot return/ we
must
fix carlito's leg/ he must be able to stand up/
when he poets his black black language/
    the raggae of *america libre*
the hot side of the new way/ the bottom of the future/
does have rhythm/ *el ritmo*

i must remember to remind my poet friends in America /
to keep matches in their houses/ i must remember that
  everywhere
nothing can be taken for granted/
        not yr thoughts. not yr beliefs.
they go with you/

or you burn them behind you/
Criminal/ huh? to watch fire eat love of what you come from/
        what you want/ Necessary for the children/
we can always remember/ but if we burn with the poems/ who
shall tell the children/ why
el salvador

We Need a God Who Bleeds Now

we need a god who bleeds now
a god whose wounds are not
some small male vengeance
some pitiful concession to humility
a desert swept with dryin marrow in honor of the lord

we need a god who bleeds
spreads her lunar vulva & showers us in shades of scarlet
thick & warm like the breath of her
our mothers tearing   to let us   in
this place breaks open
like our mothers bleeding
the planet is heaving   mourning our ignorance
the moon tugs the seas
to hold her/ to hold her
embrace swelling hills/ i am
not wounded i am bleeding to life

we need a god who bleeds now
whose wounds are not the end of anything

New World Coro

our language   is tactile
colored & wet
our tongues speak
these words
we dance
these words
sing em like we mean it/
            do it to em stuff drag punch & cruise it
to em/ live it/ the poem/
our visions are our own
our truth no less violent than necessary
to make
our daughters' dreams
as real as mensis
&
the earth hums some song of her own . . .
cuz
we have a daughter/ mozambique
we have a son/ angola
our twins
salvador & johannesburg/ cannot speak
the same language
but we fight the same old men/ in the new world
we are so hungry for the morning
we're trying to feed our children the sun
but a long time ago/ we boarded ships/ locked in
depths of seas our spirits/ kisst the earth
on the atlantic side of nicaragua costa rica
our lips traced the edges of cuba puerto rico
charleston & savannah/ in haiti

we embraced &
made children of the new world
but old men spit on us/ shackled our limbs
old men spit on us/shackled our limbs
for but a minute . . .
you'll see us in luanda or the rest of us in chicago.

From Okra to Greens /
A Different Kinda Love Story

to
Langston Hughes
& Zora Neale Thurston
for
bonnie & cal, wopo & peter
Zaki & a secret

Crooked Woman / Okra Meets Greens
in Strange Circumstances

the woman dont stand up
straight
aint never stood up
straight/ always bent
some which a way
crooked   turned abt
slanted sorta toward
a shadow of herself
seems like she
tryin to get all in the
ground/ wit the death
of her
somethin always on her
shoulders/ pushin
her outta herself
cuttin at her limbs
a wonder she cd
stand at all/ seein
how she waz all curled over herself

a greetin sent her chin
neath her arm/ a
smile chased her neck
tween her legs/
waznt just she cdnt stand up straight/
she cdnt
hardly keep somebody
else's body outta hers

& since everyone cd
see/ immediately/ this
child always bends over
always twists
round herself to
keep from standin up
folks wd just go play
wit her/ get they kicks
watchin the crooked lady
do her thing/ & her bones
gotta crackin
shatterin/ mutilatin
themselves til she
waz lookin so weird
to herself she
locked herself up in
a closet/ where she
met a man/ she musta made up/
cuz he didnt know what a stood
up straight man felt like/ &

in the dark
they curled round/ each other til
nobody cd tell anymore/ what to
get outta the way of/ & they
never once spoke/
of their condition.

From Okra to Greens / A Different Love Poem /
We Need a Change

i haveta turn my television down sometimes cuz
i cant stand to have white people/ shout at me/
sometimes i turn it off
cuz i cant look at em in my bedroom either/
being so white/
that's why i like/ greens/
they cdnt even smell you/ wdnt know what you taste like
without sneakin/ got no
idea you shd be tingled wit hot sauce & showered wit vinegar
yr pot liquor spread on hot rolls

i gotta turn the tv off cuz the white people
keep playing games/ & followin presidents on vacation at the war
there's too much of a odor problem on the tv too/ which
brings me back to greens

i remember my grandma at the market pickin turnips
collards kale & mustards/ to mix-em up/ drop a ½ a strick a lean
in there wit some ham hock & oh my whatta life/
i lived in her kitchen/ wit greens i cd recollect
yes the very root of myself
        the dirt & lil bugs i looked for in the fresh collards/
        turnin each leaf way so slow/ under the spicket/ watchin
        lil mounds of dirt fall down the drain
i done a good job
grandma tol me/ got them greens just ready for the pot
& you know/ wdnt no white man on the tv/
talkin loud n formal make no sense of the miracle
a good pot a greens on a friday nite cd make to me
that's the only reason i turn em off the tv

cant stand they gossipin abt the news/ sides they dont
never like the criminals & enemies i like anyway
that's why i like GREENS/ i know how to cook em
& i sure can dream gd/ soppin up the pot liquor
& them peppers/

Synecdoche / Asbury Park in October

all the bldgs fell thru
the earth got lil
our smiles swallowed the sky

a blue space opened tween
steel/ i lay on you

synecdoche

clouds we cd walk on
shadows race behind
pickin up what's left

In the Blueness / Says Greens

in the middle of the nite
is a blue thing
a blue thing in the nite
which covers me
makes music
like leaves that havent shown/
themselves   &
when i dont know where i am
when i dont know when i'll see you
what time it is
i lay
in the middle of the nite
covered up with   this   blueness
this memory of you

some men's eyes see hazel

mine see/ blue
sometimes it moves/ actually rocks
so even paris is not quiet
for me/ i linger by the seine
un homme noir
bein blue like the velvet hips
of river biguine for me
sway in the thickness
air on my arms
holdin me in from the nite i cd
enter with you
in the blueness
the forever weight of yr arms/
mine filled with sky

here i am carryin yr lips
yr tune now/ how you sing me
sometimes i even see clouds run
long like sea/ throw me like waves
throw me like wind/ make our breath
like the earth turnin/
never stoppin never hummin
but oh so loud

Okra to Greens Again (Special Delivery)

what language is it in
when my bed is/ too big cuz yr not in it
how cd i say
my synapses remember where yr lips
linger/ unaccompanied bach/ sometimes you
are angolan freedom songs/ we take all
confusions & raggae it/ tosh marley & wailer/ it
we stroll in our own convers all-stars/ in
london & são paulo/ but what language is it
big enough/ to say yr name

how many colors is the sound of you put to
coral skies/ dusk/ in amber & midnite reds/
if i say yr name wd the words roll like pomegranates
from everyone's mouth/ what language fits our needs
we are so far gone/ we dont know sanskrit
i dont want a saxophone/ i like greens
say how to reach you so i am clear/
you'd know pearl harbor day/ bastille day/ the
day they invaded cambodia/ is known to you/
all that death/ all the bleedin & screams/ are clear/
say how to reach you with love/ i am like air
now/ everywhere/ speakin/ whispers behind yr back
around the corner/ talkin abt you/ upstairs
in hushes/ yr name/ i stop you outside
deux maggots/ i say simply/
darling/ give me yr tongue

Fiction / Non-Fiction (Okra's Intellect Addresses Greens' Mind)

i dreamed myself in a house of yr paintings
fore you even said diagonally yes
yrs/ mine   you/ me/ this cant be simple
this is non-fiction
most of the world is make-believe & predictable

our latitudes & longitudes have other names
fiction/ non-fiction
you understand all this/ where did the question go?
he's lost/ in the office of protocol/ check with me
for verification/ my fiction file is in gd shape
i know a lotta novelists who stock up my drawers with
tales to be put away/ song writers who are mute &
tone deaf/ leave their lyrics in the milkcan outside/
somewhere in l.a. private security guards stop motorists
& force em to pick up rumors/ non-fictionally
i'm harder to reach

you cd try direct
when i'm vulnerable & survivin
i get each moment back/ i want to know
what we make
in the world/ survivin us/ makes us
non-fiction/ unless yr holdin back
then you are fiction & i am a plot
so my silence is a kind of gratitude
how often am i understood if i open my mouth
we give each other empty paper bags & ticket stubs
we've been someplaces or are going
this is not camp

this is a wide open hand/ unsettled unclaimed
in the hinterlands of ordinary/ we cd homestead it
we cd parcel it off to former levittowners
we cd put a hold on it/ we cd save it til the next time
we cd burrow our feet in soil & gather up sky wine & music

you know whatta breeze is at twilight in autumn
the horizon lays out in violet & sepia
jets of orange wisk thru our hands
that's why my neck gets so hot when you touch me
the last heavy breaths of day belong to us
non-fiction/

Okra to Greens: A Historical Perspective of Sound / Downtown

i thought i might be in slug's
pharoah waz singin
though he didnt beat his
chest
carnival rolled outta brooklyn thru the snow
& soho/ right up 7th avenue south
with our wintry american version of the jump-up
pharoah did know the sun
& tabo screamed over & over
6 tenor players filled the front row
the battles of the horns to commence
but i know this isn't slug's
cuz lee morgan's blood doesnt dot the sawdust
ayler's echoes cant be heard in the john &
sun-ra doesnt work here mondays
i'm not 19 years old/ in tie-dyed jeans
& pink satin/ watchin 3rd street burn down lil by lil
while the yng ones with mouth pieces & brushes
wait to sit in/ this isn't slug's cuz death seems
so far away/ not boomer's where death is sold in packages
it's ten years later/ & the changes are transcribed

Okra to Greens / An Aside on Amsterdam Avenue

spose i say i know yr leafy
you come in 5 different tastes/ yr edges vary
you have seasons of yr own choosin/ spose
the distance from yr collard to yr mustard
is same as from the width of my field
you know the incidence of greens overdose
is unfortunately internationally unknown
this condition is not due to pesticides war
land-fill overflow or legionnaire's disease
greens overdose might not ever be reported
/feels too good/ most victums smile
without knowing why/ but i know i gotta
o.d. of greens/ i'm sufferin so
my pods are gleamin/ ready to jump out
the vertical/ into the greens diagonal
oh
greens plant yrself which ever angle suits you
if yr wearing yr grey tie & the doc shoes/
come this way & bring me something for my blood pressure.

Revelations (The Night Greens Went Off with that
Hussy, Rutabaga)

when you disappeared
the night sat in my mouth
like a rush of a holler
how i dug my feet into the sidewalk
when mama tried to take me to the new school
how i refused to understand freedom rides
& cheap lunch counters too good for me
raw yolk across my forehead
catsup streamin from my temples
a parody of my blood
creepin thru the furrows of my lips
tastin so much like yr tongue

when you disappeared
a tremendous silence shook
my body til my bones split
i hadta grab my sinews from the mouths of bats

none of the nice boys wd dance with me
my hair turned back
i looked like the child found in
the chicken coop after 13 years
i knew no language
my fingers had never held bread
i cd not walk

when you disappeared
the moon cracked in a ugly rupture
fell a cursin for the night to catch her

From Okra to Greens: A Personal Invitation
(Reconciliation in Casablanca)

wd you like to make love tonite
landscapes can be tawdry
but the horizon at tamaris hasn't known a cheap moment
come with me to the *kasbah* or the Tin Palace
but wd you like to make love tonite
something happened on lenox/ the train came
you know what i mean/ it waznt the A train though
ellington waz looking good in brooklyn & it waznt
the coney island express with the horses ferris wheels
& junkies on the fallin boardwalks/ but the train did come
& it waz good cuz i waz cold

wd you like to make love tonite

there's a place & tony davis doesnt work there
but he gave me a lullaby/ you cd hear it
between blue brown walls i call my own
where butterflies & great ladies take respite/ you
cd rest on flowers of silk/ where i wanna make love
with you so all the trains & vamps/
my runs & songs
the steeplechase hawker/ intervals of major & doubly
augmented sighs/ the cafe in knesset where the sun makes
meat hotter than an oven/ even the angolan exiles in lisbon
cd drink with us again/ if you were to hold me tonite
everywhere we've been wd lay on me so
i might only kiss you/ like the night all we did waz kiss
all night long/ but see/ i really wanna make love tonite
how we live our lives/ so we do it all the time

Rise Up Fallen Fighters (Okra Takes Up with a Rastafari Man / She Cant Hold Back / She Say Smilin')

i've been married to bob marley
for at least 17 years
but i usedta call him smokey robinson
it's hard to remember i
waz underage at the time of our union &
changed my birthdate
so much i cant count the years
only the satisfaction

bob marley is my husband
whether our marriage is legal has to do
with where you live & if you think highly
of haile selassie/ the lion of judah
my children are hiding in toco forest
they swing on their rasta red har/ climbin
jungle jims of lapis under the supervision
of the good colored men from uranus/
where all colored men are kindergarten teachers/
where they sing my husband's songs
where we exodus-ed outta here
where natural mystics
be jammin alla time &
they be raining joy on everybody house
i tell you no lie

bob marley take care of me
cuz he wanna give me some love
been knockin on my door three year
& he still here for sure
he jump

he scream
he shake he head
he close he eye
he be in the promised land
he wait for me on star
he blaze
he sing
he wanna jam it wit me &
he dont wait in vain
he in the movement of the people
he jump
he scream
he shake he head
he close he eye
he head twirl from london to canal street
he braid fall from the sun
he see me
he lay his mark here
i reach for the world
he give it to me
i work   i rest   i love him in the air
i cd fondle the sky
watch kingston eclipse guiltiness
in the name of the lord
the lion of judah

david's warriors
rise up rise up fallen fighters
show me the promised land
show me round the universe

our fathers' land
rise up
announce the comin of the kingdom rightful heirs
i climbin to the moon on the rasta-thruway
our father lands
risin up
the land even sing & jump
the sky want to jam all thru the day
the stars forget they weakness
& dance

rise up fallen fighters
unfetter the stars
dance with the universe
& make it ours

oh, make it/ make it ours
oh make it/ make it ours.

Bob Marley d. May 11, 1981

The Beach with Okra & Greens / On Their
Honeymoon / Banda Abao, Curaçao

it be hot   & then again not
breeze know how to cool
the burnin
when the sun force us to twitch
punctuate the air
wit alla this   the breeze she
fan our behind/ tickle the bosoms   let the music
free out out soul rush
up from waves   no matter
no matter the seaweed   tease
thru legs   make us want   make us want
to swing with the horizon
so easy   so easy   to swim to swing
to stroke hard to breathe deep
but the sun she want us   to twitch
she love to watch us sway alla sudden
throw the leg round there/ hips put so to the sun
winds like opium lovers/ the winds get in our blood
run us to the sea/ the sea she want it all
the sun she want us hot
but it be hot & then again not
the sea she want it all
& she keep comin back/ she like our toes earth tanglin
                                        wet like
but the sun she want us hot so/ but it be hot
& then again
not   cuz the sun she want it all.
& we be it/ ras man/ sun/ so . . . / hot.

ACKNOWLEDGMENTS

"Bocas: A Daughter's Geography" was originally performed (under the title "Mouths") at The Kitchen, New York City, in April 1981, with the following personnel: Ntozake Shange, Richard Lawson, Halifu Osimare, Ed Monk, and Elvia Marta. Directed by Thulani Davis, Choreography by Diane McIntyre, Set Design (drawings) by Ntozake Shange, Costumes by Marion ViCaires. Produced by John Woo in association with the Basement Workshop. It was subsequently performed as part of *Three for a Full Moon* at the Mark Taper Theater Lab in Los Angeles, produced by Madeleine Puzo.

"It Hasnt Always Been This Way/A Choreopoem" was originally performed with Sounds-In-Motion at Symphony Space, New York City, and subsequently as part of *Three for a Full Moon* at The Mark Taper Theater Lab, choreographed by Michelle Simmons, produced by Madeleine Puzo.

"From Okra to Greens/A Different Love Story" was originally performed by B.O.S.S., Barnard College, Columbia University, with Bakida Carrol, Oliver Lake, and McArthur Binion; November 1979.